With Love
To
Ujwal Sonia Grewal

from Ashal (India)
17/6/07

100% TRIED & TESTED RECIPES

100% TRIED & TESTED RECIPES

Nita Mehta

B.Sc. (Home Science), M.Sc. (Food and Nutrition), Gold Medalist

Tanya Mehta

SNAB
Publishers Pvt. Ltd.

Vegetarian

First Hardbound Edition 2006

ISBN 81-7869-111-6

Food Styling & Photography: Tanya Mehta

Layout and laser typesetting:

National Information Technology Academy
3A/3, Asaf Ali Road
New Delhi-110 002
☎ 23252948

Published by:

Publishers Pvt Ltd
3A/3 Asaf Ali Road
New Delhi-110002

Editorial and Marketing office:
E-159, Greater Kailash-II, N.Delhi-48
Tel: 91-11-23250091, 23252948, Fax: 29225218
Tel: 91-11-29214011, 29218727, 29218574
E-Mail: nitamehta@email.com, nitamehta@nitamehta.com
*Website:*http://www.nitamehta.com
Website: http://www.snabindia.com

Printed at:
BRIJBASI ART PRESS LTD.

Distributed by:
THE VARIETY BOOK DEPOT
A.V.G. Bhavan, M 3 Con Circus
New Delhi - 110 001
Tel: 23417175, 23412567; Fax: 23415335

Contributing Writers:
Subhash Mehta
Anurag Mehta

Editorial & Proofreading:
Ekta
Deepali

Price: Rs. 250/-

Introduction

Watch your weight, the delicious way!

This book has quick and light recipes – all cooked without a drop of oil. Zero Oil does not mean having to say goodbye to your favourite foods. In fact, we have transformed your favourites recipes, by making them oil free.

We are often tempted to skip meals to avoid calories. This practice is not healthy at all. We miss out on the important minerals and vitamins. These zero oil recipes include the right quality and quantity of proteins, carbohydrates, vitamins and minerals without having to add much to our calorie intake.

Following a diet can be very boring if you have to eat the same foods day after day. This book offers you a range of recipes of snacks, salads, meal time dishes of Indian, Continental, Chinese and even Thai cuisine. A section on guilt free desserts is a treat. I believe that this book shall prove very useful for heart patients as well as obese people, but the food being delicious would be a joy for all. So cut down on calories, yet not on taste by making the delicious recipes given in the book.

Nita Mehta

Nita Mehta

ABOUT THE RECIPES

WHAT'S IN A CUP?

INDIAN CUP
1 teacup = 200 ml liquid
AMERICAN CUP
1 cup = 240 ml liquid (8 oz)
The recipes in this book were tested with the Indian teacup which holds 200 ml liquid.

Contents

Snacks

Diet Cole Slaw Sandwich

Makes 2

INGREDIENTS

2 slices of brown bread

DIET COLE SLAW
4 tbsp grated cabbage (band gobhi)
4 tbsp thickly grated carrot (use the biggest holes of your grater to grate)
2 tbsp very finely chopped capsicum
1 tsp readymade mustard paste
3 tbsp curd (dahi)
1 tsp vinegar, a pinch of sugar
1 tsp tomato sauce, ¼ tsp salt and pepper, or to taste

METHOD

1 Grate cabbage & carrot. Chop capsicum finely.

2 Mix all ingredients of diet cole slaw in a bowl. Check seasonings.

3 Spread mixture on a plain slice. Place the other slice on it. Press lightly.

4 Serve plain as it is or toast in a sandwich toaster till crisp and golden brown. Cut into 2 pieces and serve.

Nugget Satay

Makes 16-18

INGREDIENTS

¾ cup nutri nugget granules - soaked in hot water for 20 minutes, strained and squeezed well
1 tsp jeera (cumin)
1 tsp ginger - garlic paste (½" piece of ginger & 4 flakes of garlic - crushed to a paste)
1 onion - chopped
1 capsicum - chopped very finely
¼ tsp haldi, ¾ tsp salt, ½ tsp red chilli powder
½ tsp garam masala, 1 tsp dhania powder (coriander powder), ¼ tsp amchoor
¼ cup readymade tomato puree
seeds of 3 chhoti illaichi (green cardamoms) - crushed
1-2 tsp lemon juice or to taste
1 green chilli - chopped finely
½ potato - boiled and grated
½ cup dry bread crumbs
few wooden or bamboo skewers/sticks

METHOD

1 Heat a kadhai, add 1 tsp jeera. Let it turn golden.

2 Add ginger-garlic paste.

3 Add onion. Cook till light brown on low heat.

4 Remove from fire. Add masala - haldi, garam masala, red chilli powder, dhania powder, amchoor and salt.

5 Return to fire. Add tomato puree and chhoti ilaichi powder. Stir.

6 Add nuggets & stir for about 10 minutes. Add 4 tbsp water and cook for 1 more minute.

7 Add capsicums and cook further for 2 minutes. Remove from fire. Cool.

8 Add lemon juice and green chillies.

9 Add the potatoes and bread crumbs.

10 Flatten a ball of this mixture on a wooden skewer. Do not keep the mixture on the skewer too broad as it falls, if done so. Cook from both sides on a nonstick pan till brown specs appear. Serve with some tomato ketchup or hari chutney.

Cornflakes Chaat

Serves 4

INGREDIENTS

1 cup cornflakes (Kellog's)
½ cup kala or kabuli channas - boiled (1½ cups)
1 boiled potato - chopped
2 tomatoes - chopped
1 kheera (cucumber) - cut into ½" pieces without peeling
3-4 tbsp anaar ke dane (fresh pomegranate), some chopped coriander

MEETHI CHUTNEY
4 tbsp sugar, ¼ cup water
½ tsp salt, 2 tbsp amchoor, ½ tsp red chilli powder, ½ tsp bhuna jeera

HARA DHANIA CHUTNEY
1 cup chopped coriander with stalks
1 tomato - chopped , 1 flake garlic - chopped, ½ tsp grated ginger, 1 green chilli
1 tsp lemon juice, salt and sugar to taste

BEAT TOGETHER
1 cup yogurt (dahi)
¼ tsp bhuna jeera powder (roasted cumin powder)
¼ tsp red chilli powder, ¼ tsp chaat masala
salt to taste

METHOD

1 For meethi chutney, mix all ingredients. Boil. Cook for a few minutes, stirring continuously, till slightly thick. Remove from fire and keep aside.

2 Blend all ingredients of the green chutney to a paste.

3 Beat dahi with bhuna jeera powder red chilli powder, chaat masala and salt till smooth.

4 Mix channa, potato, tomato and kheera with half of the curd in a big bowl. Transfer to a flat serving platter. Sprinkle both chutneys and keep aside. Do not mix.

5 Add little water to the remaining curd to make it of a pouring consistency.

6 Just at the time of serving, sprinkle cornflakes. Sprinkle remaining dahi, then the chutneys on it. Serve sprinkled with some anar ke dane and finely chopped coriander.

Peshawari Kebabs

Makes 12

INGREDIENTS

1 cup soya granules (nutri nugget granules)
1 cup thickly grated carrot
1 capsicum - finely chopped
2 onions - finely chopped
3 tsp ginger-garlic paste (1½" piece of ginger and 8- 9 flakes of garlic)
¾ tsp salt, ¼ tsp red chilli powder, ¼ tsp garam masala
1 cup yogurt (dahi) - hang for 20-25 minutes in a muslin cloth
4 tbsp cornflour
2 tsp chana masala
4 tbsp fresh anar ke dane (pomegranate), optional

METHOD

1 Soak soya granules in 2 cups of hot water for 15 minutes.

2 Strain. Squeeze out the water well from the soya granules. (No water should remain). You can also put the soya granules in a muslin cloth and squeeze.

3 In a nonstick kadhai add onion and cook on low heat till soft. Put ginger-garlic paste. Stir.

4 Add nuggets and stir continuously for 3- 4 minutes.

5 Add carrot. Cook for 3-4 minutes on medium heat till dry. Remove from fire. Cool and grind coarsely in a mixer.

6 Add capsicum, salt, red chilli powder and garam masala to the nugget mixture. Mix well.

7 Mix cornflour & chana masala to yogurt. Add this yogurt to the kebab mixture. Mix very well till the mixture binds well.

8 Divide the mixture into 12 equal portions and make balls.

9 Take a ball and flatten slightly. Roll the sides on a flat surface to get clean edges. Press some anar ke dane on it. Keep them in the fridge for ½ hour to set well.

10 Cook on medium heat on a greased non stick pan till light brown on both sides. Serve hot.

Papad Tacos

A good substitute for chip and dip
Makes 16

INGREDIENTS

4 medium sized papads (roasting ones) - cut each into 4 pieces with a pair of scissors
some readymade salsa
a few lettuce leaves - washed, pat-dried and torn into 2" pieces

VEGETABLES
¼ cup finely chopped cucumber (kheera)
¼ cup finely chopped cabbage (bandgobhi)
¼ cup grated carrot (gajar)
½ capsicum - chopped finely
¼ tsp salt or to taste
½ tsp white pepper or to taste

SOUR CREAM
½ cup (100 gm) fresh thick curd - hang for 30 minutes in a muslin cloth
a pinch of salt and white pepper or to taste
1 tbsp chopped coriander (hara dhania)
½ green chili - deseeded and chopped

METHOD

1 Mix all ingredients of sour cream.

2 Roast each piece of papad. Immediately wrap the hot papad on the edge of the fat side of the belan (rolling pin) to make a cup of the papad. Leave aside to cool and become crisp. You can do this well in advance and store in an air tight tin.

3 Mix vegetables with sour cream to make salad. Check salt and pepper. Keep in a separate bowl. Put salsa in another bowl.

4 At serving time, place a lettuce leaf on papad, fill it with some salad, top with salsa. Serve immediately.

Bread Dahi Vadas

Prepare at least 1 hour before serving, for the bread to soak the dahi.

Serves 8

INGREDIENTS

6 slices of fresh bread, preferably whole wheat bread
2 cups thick curd (of toned milk) - beat till smooth
¾ tsp bhuna jeera powder (roasted cumin powder)
½ tsp red chilli powder
¼ tsp kala namak (black salt)
1 tsp salt, a pinch of powdered sugar, or to taste

OTHER INGREDIENTS
1 tbsp finely chopped fresh coriander
2 green chillies - deseeded and chopped finely
2 tsp ginger juliennes/match stick like pieces
some hari chutney and meethi chutney (see recipe on page 12)
2-3 tbsp red anaar ke dane (fresh pomegranate), optional

METHOD

1 Whip curd. Add bhuna jeera, red chilli powder, kala namak, salt and sugar to taste. Keep the raita aside.

2 Cut small rounds from all bread slices.

3 Spread 2- 3 tbsp of raita in a shallow rectangular dish. Arrange half of the bread rounds over the raita.

4 Spread 1 tbsp of curd over each piece of bread. Sprinkle a pinch of chopped coriander, few chopped green chillies and 1-2 ginger juliennes on it.

5 Spread raita over the remaining bread pieces. Invert them with raita spread down on the arranged pieces on the dish.

6 Pour the left over dahi on them to cover completely.

7 With a spoon, pour the chutneys on it, in circles.

8 Garnish with bhuna jeera, red chilli powder, some ginger juliennes and red anar ke dane. Leave in the fridge for atleast ½ hour for the bread to soak the curd.

9 Serve with some hari chutney and also some extra imli chutney.

Semolina Surprise

Serves 6

INGREDIENTS

1 cup semolina (sooji) - roasted
¾ tsp salt
1 cup yogurt (dahi)
½ tsp oregano
1 tbsp eno fruit salt
½ carrot (gajar) - grated
2-3 tbsp chopped capsicum
4 tbsp hari chutney (see recipe on page 12)
½ tsp sugar

METHOD

1 Roast semolina in a kadhai, stirring continuously till it turns light golden and fragrant about 3- 4 minutes. Let it cool.

2 Add salt, yogurt and oregano. Mix well to get a thick batter.

3 Boil 2 cups of water in a deep pan (patila) for steaming. Place a steel colander (a steel channi with big holes) on the patila.

4 Mix eno with sooji batter and transfer half of the batter to a greased thali to get ½" thick layer.

5 Sprinkle most of the grated carrot and chopped capsicum over it. Then put drops of hari chutney with a spoon all over.

6 Pour the rest of sooji mixture on the vegetables.

7 Top with the remaining grated carrot and capsicum.

8 Place the thali on the steel colander. Cover the colander. Steam for 15-20 minutes. Check with a knife in the centre. If it comes out clean it is done. Cut into 2" triangles or square pieces.

Mushroom Croustades

Serves 2

2 hot dog buns

FILLING
9-10 mushrooms (120 gms) - chopped finely
2 small spring onions (hara pyaz) - chopped including the greens
2 tsp soya sauce, ½ tsp salt, ½ tsp pepper or to taste

METHOD

1 Cut each hot dog bun into half lengthwise. Scoop out the soft center portion with a knife, leaving a border.

2 Grill all the 4 pieces in a preheated oven till crisp.

3 For the filling, heat a pan, add white of spring onions. Cook for 2 minutes, stirring. Add mushrooms, cook for 3-4 minutes or till dry.

4 Add soya sauce, salt and pepper. Add greens of spring onion. Mix. Remove from fire.

5 Spoon this hot mixture into grilled hollowed bread croustade. Serve whole or cut into two pieces.

Curd Triangles

Serves 4-5

INGREDIENTS

1 cup thick curd (prepared from toned milk) - hang for 1-2 hours
3-4 tbsp shredded cabbage, 2-3 tbsp grated carrot
1 green chilli - deseeded and finely chopped, salt and pepper to taste
2 tbsp green mint or coriander chutney (optional), see page 12
6 slices bread, preferably brown bread

METHOD

1 Beat hung curd in a bowl till smooth.

2 Add cabbage, carrot, green chilli, salt and pepper. Mix well. Add a little extra salt, otherwise the spread tastes bland.

3 Spread the curd mix generously on a slice.

4 Spread some chutney on another slice. Place the chutney slice, with the chutney side down on the curd slice. Press well.

5 Grill in a sandwich toaster or in the oven on the wire rack till browned and crisp.

6 Cut into 4 triangles and serve hot. Repeat with the other 4 slices. Serve.

Veggie Pick ups

Serves 10-12

8 soya chunks (nutri nuggets)
1 onion - cut into 8 pieces and separated
6 paneer cubes of ¾ "
8-10 medium flat florets of broccoli with little stalk
6 - 8 medium flat florets of cauliflower
8 small baby corns, 8 small mushrooms
1 green capsicum - cut into ¾" squares pieces
1 yellow capsicum- cut into ¾" squares pieces
2 tomatoes - pulp removed and cubed
4 tbsp all-in-one stir fry sauce
1 tsp sesame seeds (til), a few tooth picks

MARINADE (MIX TOGETHER)
2 tbsp cornflour
1 tsp salt and ¾ tsp white pepper, or to taste
1 tsp garlic paste (2-3 flakes of garlic- crushed to a paste)
½ tsp red chilli flakes
 4 tbsp tomato sauce, 1 tsp soya sauce
2 tsp red chilli sauce

METHOD

1 Boil 5-6 cups water with 1 tsp salt, 1 tsp sugar and 1 tsp lemon juice. Add broccoli, cauliflower, baby corns and mushrooms. Remove from fire. Leave them in hot water for 2-3 minutes. Remove veggies from water with a strainer. Keep aside. Boil water again. Add nuggets and boil for 3-4 minutes or till soft. Remove from water. Squeeze well and keep aside.

2 Marinate the soya chunks, paneer, the blanched veggies and capsicum (except tomatoes) in the marinade mixture. Keep aside till serving time.

3 Heat a non stick pan. Reduce flame. Add the marinated ingredients and saute for 5 minutes, keeping them in a single layer in the pan.

4 Add all-in-one stir fry sauce.

5 Add the tomatoes. Remove from fire.

6 Spread out the veggies in the pan and sprinkle some sesame seeds.

7 Skewer a tomato, soya ball and lastly a capsicum piece on the tooth pick. In the same way replace the soya chunk with blanched veggies or paneer. Serve hot.

Salads and Soups

Tangy Carrot Soup

Serves 4

2 big (250 gms) carrots - peeled and chopped
1 potato - peeled and chopped
1 onion - chopped, 8-10 peppercorns (saboot kali mirch)
1" piece ginger - chopped, 4 cups vegetable stock or water
juice of one orange or ½ cup ready-made orange juice
2 tbsp chopped coriander, ¾ tsp salt or to taste, ¼ tsp pepper

METHOD

1 Saute onion, peppercorns and ginger in a non stick pan till onions start to change colour.

2 To it add carrots and potato. Stir for 2-3 minutes on low flame. Add water. Bring to a boil. Simmer on low flame for 10-15 minutes till the vegetables get cooked. Remove from fire.

3 Cool and grind to a puree in a blender. Strain the vegetable puree.

4 Add orange juice, coriander, salt and pepper. Boil. Serve hot or cold.

Spinach & Mushroom Soup

Serves 3-4

INGREDIENTS

1 cup roughly chopped spinach
6 mushrooms - sliced very finely (paper thin slices)
2 cups milk, 1 flake garlic - crushed, 2 cups water mixed with 2 tbsp cornflour
4-6 peppercorns (saboot kali mirch) - crushed, 1 tsp salt, or to taste, 1 tsp lemon juice

METHOD

1 Boil chopped spinach with milk. Cook uncovered, for about 5 minutes or till spinach softens. Remove from fire. Cool. Strain the spinach and reserve the milk.

2 Put spinach in a blender with a little milk and roughly blend. Do not blend too much. Keep spinach puree aside.

3 Heat a pan, add garlic & mushrooms and saute for 3-4 minutes. Add the spinach puree and the milk kept aside.

4 Add 2 cups water mixed with 2 tbsp cornflour. Stir till it boils. Cook stirring frequently for 3-4 minutes. Add salt and freshly crushed pepper.

5 Remove from fire. Add lemon juice to taste. Serve hot.

Herbed Green Pea Soup

Serves 4

¾ cup shelled peas (matar), ½ cup chopped potato (1 potato)
1 seasoning cube (maggi or knorr), 1 onion - chopped, 1" piece of ginger - grated
1" stick dalchini (cinnamon), 1 tsp jeera (cumin seeds)
¾ cup chopped spinach (palak), 1 tbsp mint leaves (poodina)
1 tbsp coriander (hara dhania)
¼ tsp salt, ½ tsp pepper, or to taste

METHOD

1 Boil peas, potatoes, onion, ginger, dalchini, jeera and 5 cups of water in a pan. Cook for 8-10 minutes.

2 When potatoes are cooked, add spinach, mint, coriander and 1 cup water. Cook uncovered for 3-4 minutes till the spinach turns tender.

3 Add salt, pepper and seasoning cube. Mix, add 1 cup water. Give 1-2 boils. Check salt and remove from fire.

4 Serve the soup piping hot with garlic bread.

Lauki and Tomato Soup

Serves 4

INGREDIENTS

4 (300) gm tomatoes - roughly chopped
125 gms lauki or ghiya (bottle gourd) - peeled and chopped (1 cup)
½" piece ginger, 5-6 saboot kali mirch (peppercorns)
1 onion - chopped, ¾ tsp salt, ¼ tsp pepper or to taste
a pinch of sugar, fresh coriander to garnish

METHOD

1 In a pressure cooker, boil the tomatoes, ghiya, ginger, saboot kali mirch and onion with 4 cups of water to give 1 whistle. Keep on low flame for 4-5 minutes. Remove from fire.

2 Cool and puree in a blender. Strain the puree. Boil soup. Add the salt, pepper and sugar. Add fresh coriander.

3 Simmer for a few minutes. Serve hot.

Note: For variation, instead of ghiya one may use 2 tbsp of moong dhuli dal and juice of half a lemon.

Fruity Salad in Orange Dressing

Serves 3- 4

INGREDIENTS

½ cup cubed cabbage
1 carrot - cubed (½ cup)
½ onion - cubed (¼ cup chopped)
1 tomato - cubed
½ cup halved or chopped grapes or strawberries
½ cup orange segments (pieces)

ORANGE DRESSING
¼ cup orange juice (fresh or ready made)
1 tsp lemon juice
2-3 flakes garlic - crushed, ½ tsp oregano
½ tsp salt and pepper, or to taste

METHOD

1 Mix all fruits and vegetables in a large bowl. Chill in the fridge till serving time.

2 Mix all ingredients of the orange dressing in a bottle. Close cap and shake well to mix. Keep aside.

3 An hour before serving, pour the dressing over the fruit and vegetable mixture in the bowl.

4 Toss lightly with two forks. Add more salt and pepper if desired.

5 Refrigerate till serving time.

Broccoli & Bean Salad in Mustard Dressing

Serves 4

INGREDIENTS

VEGETABLES
100 gm (20-25) tender French beans
1 small (250 gm) broccoli (hari gobhi)
1 tomato or 3-4 strawberries

MUSTARD DRESSING
2 tsp mustard paste
½ tsp peppercorns (saboot kali mirch) - crushed
½ tsp salt, 2 tsp curd
juice of 1 large lemon (2½-3 tbsp)
2-3 flakes garlic - sliced finely
1 tsp water

METHOD

1. Mix all ingredients of the dressing together in a small bowl.

2. Thread beans & cut into 1½" long pieces.

3. Cut broccoli into medium florets with a little stalk.

4. Cut strawberries or tomato lengthwise into slices. Remove pulp from tomatoes.

5. Boil 4-5 cups water with 2 tsp salt and 2 tsp sugar.

6. Add beans to the boiling water. As soon as the boil returns, keep the beans boiling for 1 minute.

7. Add broccoli. Remove from fire. Leave the vegetables in hot water for 2 minutes.

8. Strain the vegetables. Refresh by taking them out of cold water. Leave in the strainer to drain out all the water.

9. Pat dry the vegetables on a cloth napkin and transfer them to a mixing bowl.

10. Add the sliced tomatoes or strawberries.

11. Add the dressing to the vegetables. Toss to mix well. Serve cold.

Baked Tomato Cups

Tomatoes stuffed with cooked apples, tempered with South Indian ingredients.

Serves 6

INGREDIENTS

6 medium sized firm tomatoes - halved
1½ tsp rai (mustard seeds)
6-8 leaves curry leaves (patta)
2 medium onions - chopped
4 tbsp chopped capsicum
2 medium apples - finely chopped
½ tsp amchoor
4 tbsp fresh brown bread crumbs (churn 1 bread in a mixer to get fresh crumbs)
½ tsp salt, ¼ tsp pepper
a few coriander leaves (hara dhania)

METHOD

1 Cut tomatoes into 2 pieces. Scoop the pulp and sprinkle salt. Keep them inverted on a plate.

2 Stir rai in a pan on low heat till roasted. Add the onions. Cook for 1 minute and add the curry patta and capsicum.

3 Remove from flame. Add apples, salt, pepper, amchoor and bread crumbs. Mix well.

4 Fill mixture in the tomatoes. To make the tomatoes stand upright, cut a thin slice from the base of the tomatoes.

5 At serving time, bake at 200°C for 10-12 minutes til soft but firm.

6 Garnish each with a coriander leaf.

Dieter's Creamy Salad

Serves 6

INGREDIENTS

2½ cups toned milk
½ cup curd or juice of ½ lemon to curdle the milk
1 cup thick curd - hang for ½ hour in a muslin cloth
2 tsp sugar
few drops of tobasco sauce or ½ tsp mustard paste
½ carrot - finely cubed and boiled till crisp tender
¼ cup boiled peas (matar)
½ capsicum - cut into thin strips
½ cup grapes - halved
1 apple - cut into ½" pieces without peeling
½ cup cucumber (kheera) - cut into ½" pieces
2-3 beans - cut into ½" pieces, boiled till crisp tender

METHOD

1 Boil milk. Reduce flame and add curd or lemon juice to curdle the milk. As soon as the milk curdles and paneer is formed remove from flame and strain through a muslin cloth. Leave paneer in the cloth for at least ½ hour till the water (whey) gets drained.

2 Blend paneer, curd, sugar and tobasco or mustard in a mixer till smooth.

3 Remove from mixer to a bowl. Add salt and pepper.

4 Mix most of the fruits and vegetables in the curd-paneer mixture, keeping aside some for garnishing. Transfer to a serving bowl. Chill. Serve.

Curries

Paneer in Red Gravy

Serves 4

INGREDIENTS

250 gm paneer - cut into 1" cubes
6 (500 gm) tomatoes - each cut into 4 pieces or 1 cup readymade tomato puree
4-5 flakes garlic and 1" piece ginger - ground to a paste (1½ tsp ginger-garlic paste)
1 tbsp kasoori methi (dry fenugreek leaves), 2 tsp tomato ketchup
½ tsp jeera (cumin seeds), 2 tsp dhania powder, ½ tsp garam masala
1 tsp salt, or to taste, ½ tsp red chilli powder, preferably degi mirch
½-1 cup milk, approx.
½ cup water

METHOD

1 Boil tomatoes in ½ cup water. Cover and cook on low heat for 4-5 minutes till tomatoes turn soft. Remove from fire and cool. Grind the tomatoes along with the water to a smooth puree.

2 Heat jeera in a kadhai. When it turns golden, add ginger-garlic paste.

3 Add the above tomato puree or use the readymade tomato puree. Cook till puree turns dry.

4 Add kasoori methi & tomato ketchup.

5 Add masalas - dhania powder, garam masala, salt and red chilli powder. Mix well for a few seconds. Cook till the masala turns little dry.

6 Add water. Boil. Simmer on low heat for 4-5 minutes. Remove from fire. Keep aside to cool for about 5 minutes.

7 Add enough milk to the cold masala to get a thick curry, mix gently (Remember to add milk only after the masala is no longer hot, to prevent the milk from curdling. After adding milk, heat curry on low heat).

8 Add the paneer cubes. Keep aside till serving time.

9 To serve heat on low flame, stirring continuously till just about to boil.

10 To serve transfer to a serving dish. Swirl a tsp of thin curd over the gravy.

Shabnam Curry

Musroom, peas and corn in a curry.
Serves 4

INGREDIENTS

100 gm mushrooms - cut into 4 pieces
½ cup peas - frozen or boiled
¼ cup corn kernels (bhutte ke daane) - frozen or boiled
¾ cup dahi and 1 tsp cornflour - beaten together till smooth
2 onions - very finely chopped
½ tsp kalonji (nigella seeds), ½ tsp jeera, 1 tsp ginger-garlic paste
2 tomatoes - blanched, pureed and sieved
3 tbsp tomato puree
1 tsp kasoori methi (dry fenugreek leaves)
½ tsp red chilli powder, ½ tsp haldi, ½ tsp garam masala, ¼ tsp salt, 2 laung
2 laung (cloves) and seeds of 2 chhoti illaichi (green cardamom)- crushed together

METHOD

1 To blanch mushrooms, boil 2 cups water with 1 tsp salt, 1 tsp sugar and 1 tbsp lemon juice. Add mushrooms and boil for 1 minute. Add peas. Boil again. Strain and keep aside.

2 Heat a kadhai. Add kalonji and jeera. Stir till jeera turn brown.

3 Add onions and stir on medium heat. Add 3-4 tbsp water and cook till light brown.

4 Add blanched, pureed and sieved tomatoes and tomato puree. Cook, stirring till it almost dries up.

5 Add ginger-garlic paste. Stir for 2 minutes.

6 Add kasoori methi, red chilli, haldi, salt & garam masala. Stir for 2-3 minutes.

7 Remove from fire. Wait for 2 minutes. Add curd beaten with cornflour. Stir for 1-2 minutes on low heat.

8 Add blanched mushrooms. Cook for 2 minutes.

9 Add water (about 1½ cups). Stir. Bring to a boil. Simmer without covering for 5 minutes.

10 Add peas and corn kernels. Bring to a boil.

11 Add crushed laung and chhoti illaichi. Cook for 1 minute. Check seasonings. Remove from fire.

Kaali Dal or Rajmah

Serves 6

INGREDIENTS

1½ cups rajmah (red kidney beans) or kaali dal (saboot urad)
1 large onion - grated
8-10 flakes garlic - crushed
2 tsp salt, or to taste
¾ tsp red chilli powder
½ cup ready made tomato puree (read note)
1 tsp jeera powder (cumin powder)
2 tsp tandoori masala or ¾ tsp garam masala
1" piece ginger - cut into thin long pieces

METHOD

1 Soak the rajmah or kaali dal overnight.

2 Pressure cook the rajmah or kaali dal with one grated onion, crushed garlic, salt, red chilli powder and enough water (about 5 cups) to give 1 whistle and keep on low flame for 20 minutes.

3 Remove from fire. After the pressure drops, mash it lightly with a masher or ladle (karchhi).

4 Add tomato puree, jeera powder and tandoori masala or garam masala. Pressure cook for 2 or 3 whistles. Remove from fire. Let the pressure drop by itself.

5 If it is rajmah it is ready to serve. For kali dal, add ½ cup milk to get the right consistency. Cook for 3-4 minutes on low heat. Serve hot garnished with some ginger juliennes.

Note: You can use fresh homemade tomato puree also. Churn 3 tomatoes in a mixer. Cook puree in a separate pan till dry and then add to the dal or rajmah.

Mirch ~ Makai Ka Salan

Green thick chillies and baby corn in a tamarind based gravy. If thick green chillies are not available, use the regular ones.

Serves 4

INGREDIENTS

6-8 (50 gm) baby corns - cut lengthwise into 2 pieces
1-2 big thick green chillies - cut into thin strips & deseeded or 3-4 whole green chillies
¼ - ½ cup cabbage - cut into 1" squares
¼ tsp of haldi (turmeric powder)
1 tsp dhania powder, ½ tsp garam masala
a lemon sized ball of imli - soak in ¼ cup water and extract juice
½ cup tomato puree, 1 tbsp wheat flour (atta)
1 tsp salt, or to taste, ¼ tsp red chilli powder

BOIL TOGETHER FOR 4-5 MINUTES AND GRIND TO A PASTE
2 large onions - roughly chopped
½" piece chopped ginger (1 tsp), ¼ cup water

FOR GARNISHING
coloured bell peppers - cut into thin fingers

TO SERVE
boiled rice

METHOD

1 Heat a pan. Add babycorns, green chillies and cabbage. Saute for 4-5 minutes till brown specs appear. Remove from fire and keep aside.

2 For masala, heat a pan. Add the prepared boiled onion paste. Cook on low heat till light brown for about 7-8 minutes.

3 Add haldi, dhania and garam masala. Stir for a minute.

4 Add tomato puree. Cook for 5 minutes on low heat till dry.

5 Add wheat flour & bhuno continuously for 2-3 minutes.

6 Add 1½ cups water, tamarind juice (according to your taste) and boil. Add salt and red chilli powder to taste. Add babycorns. Simmer on low flame for 5 minutes.

7 At serving time, heat the curry and add green chillies & cabbage. Remove from heat immediately. Garnish with coloured bell peppers and serve with boiled rice.

Note: Choose green chillies which are thick, big and light green, as the small, dark green ones are hotter. Remember, to deseed them. After deseeding them, tap them gently to remove all the seeds.

Paalak Paneer

Serves 4

INGREDIENTS

½ kg paalak (spinach), choose a bundle with smaller leaves
1 moti illaichi (brown cardamom)
2-3 laung (cloves), 3-4 saboot kali mirch (peppercorns)
3 onions - chopped, 1" piece ginger - chopped
4-6 flakes garlic - chopped, 1 green chilli - chopped
1 tbsp kasoori methi (dried fenugreek leaves)
¾ tsp garam masala, ½ tsp red chilli powder
¼ tsp amchoor, 1¼ tsp salt, or to taste
2 tomatoes - chopped
100 gms paneer (cottage cheese) - cut into 1" cubes

METHOD

1 Break paalak leaves into small pieces. Discard stalks. Wash leaves in plenty of water. Keep aside to drain.

2 In a kadhai add moti illaichi, laung and saboot kali mirch.

3 Add onions and stir on low heat till light brown.

4 Add ginger, garlic and green chillies. Mix well.

5 Add kasoori methi, garam masala, red chilli powder, amchoor and salt.

6 Add chopped tomatoes. Cook for 3-4 minutes, till well blended.

7 Add spinach and cook uncovered for 10-12 minutes on low flame. Remove from fire. Cool.

8 Blend the cooled mixture along with ½ cup water, just for a few seconds, to a coarse paste. Do not grind it too finely.

9 Boil 1 cup water and add the spinach paste to it. Simmer, uncovered for 4-5 minutes.

10 Mix paneer pieces in the cooked spinach. Give it one boil. Simmer for 2-3 minutes till paneer turns soft. Transfer to a serving dish.

Dhingri Matar

Potatoes in a semi dry sauce prepared from the juice of fresh pomegranate.

Serves 4

INGREDIENTS

1 cup shelled peas (matar)
25 gms dhingri (dry white mushrooms) - washed and soaked overnight
3 medium sized tomatoes
4 laung (cloves), 1 stick dalchini (cinnamon)
1 tsp salt, or to taste, ¼ tsp haldi powder
some chopped coriander

GRIND TO A PASTE TOGETHER (ONION & CHILLI PASTE)
1 onion, 1" piece ginger, 6-7 flakes garlic
2 dry, red chillies (whole) - deseeded & soaked in water for 15 minutes

ROAST LIGHTLY ON A TAWA AND GRIND TO A POWDER
1 tbsp saboot dhania (coriander seeds)
1 tsp jeera (cumin seeds), seeds of 2 moti illaichi (brown cardamoms)

METHOD

1 Wash dhingri in 2-3 changes of water. Soak dhingri overnight. Next morning wash again in 3-4 changes of water. Cut dhingri into ½" pieces (small pieces) with a knife. Discard any very hard portion, if present.

2 Lightly roast on tawa - saboot dhania, jeera and moti illaichi seeds. Cool and powder finely.

3 Put tomatoes in boiling water, boil for 2-3 minutes. Remove the skin & puree.

4 Heat a pan. Add laung and dalchini. Wait for a minute.

5 Add ground onion-chilli paste, salt and haldi powder. Stir fry till onions turn golden.

6 Add tomato puree. Cook till dry.

7 Add dhingri to the cooked masala & lower the heat & bhuno for 4-5 minutes.

8 Add peas & bhuno for another 1-2 minutes on low heat.

9 Add roasted powdered masala of jeera, dhania and moti illaichi. Mix.

10 Add enough water (about 1½ cups) to get a gravy. Boil and simmer till peas get cooked. Serve hot.

Matar Waali Kadhi

Serves 3-4

INGREDIENTS

¾ cup shelled peas (matar)
4 tbsp besan (gram flour)
1 cup curd
1 tsp garlic paste (3- 4 flakes of garlic- crushed to a paste)
1 tsp salt, or to taste
½ tsp haldi
½ tsp red chilli powder
2 moti illaichi (black cardamoms)
3-4 laung (cloves)
6-8 saboot kali mirch (black peppercorns)
½ tsp garam masala
a few curry leaves

METHOD

1 In a sauce pan boil 1 cup water with ½ tsp salt, 1 tsp sugar and 1 tsp lemon juice. Add peas. Boil for 1-2 minutes.

2 Beat curd well. Add besan and garlic to it. Mix well. Add 2 cups of water.

3 Add salt, haldi, red chilli powder, moti illaichi, laung and kali mirch.

4 Cook in a deep pan, on high flame stirring often till a boil comes. Simmer & cook for 8-10 minutes till all the frothiness goes.

5 Add the curry patta and blanched peas & cook for 2 minutes till peas turn soft.

6 Sprinkle garam masala on it. Serve.

Handi Channa

Serves 4-5   *Cal/Serving 117*

2 cups kabuli channa (chick peas)
2 moti illaichi (brown cardamoms), 3-4 laung (cloves)
1 large onion - finely chopped
1 tsp garlic paste, 1 tsp ginger paste, 1½ - 2 tsp salt, or to taste
3 tsp channa masala, ½ tsp red chilli powder
½ tsp garam masala, 4 tsp dhania powder
2 tsp bhuna jeera powder (roasted cumin powder)
3 tsp imli (tamarind) pulp or squeeze out pulp from 1" ball of tamarind

GARNISHING
1 tomato - cut into 8 pieces
1-2 green chillies - cut lengthwise into half
a few ginger juliennes (match sticks)

METHOD

1 Soak the channas overnight.

2 Next morning drain water. Put in a pressure cooker. Add 4 cups fresh water. Add finely chopped onion, moti illaichi, laung, garlic paste and ginger paste. Pressure cook to give 1 whistle and keep on low flame for 15-20 minutes.

3 After the pressure drops open the cooker. Add salt, dhania powder, channa masala, jeera powder, garam masala, black pepper, red chilli and the tamarind pulp to the cooked channas. Mash the channas a bit.

4 Again pressure cook to give 1 whistle. Remove from fire.

5 Serve hot garnished with ginger match sticks, tomatoes and green chillies.

Sarson ka Saag

Serves 6

INGREDIENTS

1 bundle (1 kg) sarson (green mustard) - choose tender leaves with tender stems
250 gm spinach or baathoo
2 shalgam (turnips) - peeled and chopped, optional
3-4 flakes garlic - finely chopped, optional
2" piece ginger - finely chopped
1 green chilli - chopped, ¾ tsp salt, or to taste
2 tbsp makki ka atta (maize flour)
1½ tsp powdered gur (jaggery)

METHOD

1 Wash and clean mustard leaves. First remove the leaves and then peel the stems, starting from the lower end and chop them finely. (Peel stems the way you string green beans). The addition of stems to the saag makes it tastier but it is important to peel the stems from the lower ends. The upper tender portion may just be chopped.

2 Chop the spinach or baathoo leaves and mix with sarson.

3 Put chopped greens with ½ cup water in a pan.

4 Chop garlic, ginger and green chilli very finely and add to the saag, add shalgam if you wish. Add salt and put it on fire and let it start heating.

5 The saag will start going down. Cover and let it cook on medium fire for 15-20 minutes. Remove from fire, cool.

6 Grind to a rough paste. Do not grind too much. Add gur, makki ka atta, ginger and green chillies to the saag and cook for 15 minutes on low heat. Serve hot with makki-ki-roti.

Kandhari Aloo

Potatoes in a semi dry sauce prepared from the juice of fresh pomegranate.
Serves 2

INGREDIENTS

3 potatoes
1 onion - grind to a paste
¼ cup tomato puree (readymade)
salt to taste
½ tsp degi mirch or red chilli powder
½ tsp kasoori methi (dry fenugreek leaves)
1 cup fresh anaar ke daane (juice & strained) - keep some for garnish
½" piece ginger - cut into match sticks or juliennes
a few coriander leaves for garnishing

METHOD

1 Boil and peel potatoes. Cut each into 4 pieces.

2 Blend anaar ke daane in a mixer. Strain nicely to get juice.

3 Cook onion paste in a kadhai on low flame till all water dries out.

4 Mix tomato puree & ½ cup water. Add this to the onions.

5 Bring it to a boil and cook till thick.

6 Add potatoes, salt and degi mirch.

7 Add anaar juice, kasoori methi & cook till it coats the potatoes.

8 Garnish with anaar ke dane, ginger juliennes and coriander leaves.

Dry Dishes

Subzian Kali Mirch

Serves 2-3

INGREDIENTS

1 tbsp grated ginger
1 onion - sliced
25 gms paneer - cut into 4-5 cubes
½ tomato - cut into thin fingers
6-7 beans - cut into 2" pieces
1 carrot - cut into round slices
2 mushrooms - cut into half
½ cup cubed cabbage (cut into 1" pieces)
1 tsp salt, pepper to taste
4 tbsp milk

TOPPING
coriander leaves
5-6 peppercorns - crushed coarsely

METHOD

1 Cut tomatoes into thin fingers.

2 Cut french beans into 2" pieces & cut carrots into round slices.

3 Boil 2 cups water and ¾ tsp salt and ½ tsp sugar.

4 Add carrots, beans, mushrooms & boil for just 1-2 minutes or till crisp tender. Refresh in cold water and keep aside.

5 Heat a kadhai & add cabbage, onions and ginger. Stir for 3-4 minutes till onion turns light brown.

6 Add beans, carrots & mushrooms. Stir for 2 minutes.

7 Add salt and pepper. Lower heat, add tomatoes and cook for 2 minutes.

8 Add paneer & milk. Remove from fire.

9 Serve sprinkled with freshly crushed pepper and coriander.

Baingan Achaari

A semi dry brinjal dish with lots of tomatoes and pickle spices.

Serves 4

INGREDIENTS

400 gms (5-6) brinjals of long thin variety
½ kg tomatoes - chopped finely
1 tsp ginger or garlic paste
15- 20 curry leaves
½ tsp haldi (turmeric powder)
½ tsp red chilli powder
1 tbsp dhania powder (coriander powder)
½ tsp salt, or to taste, ½ tsp garam masala

COLLECT TOGETHER
a pinch of hing (asafoetida)
1 tsp saunf (fennel)
½ tsp kalonji (onion seeds)
½ tsp methi dana (fenugreek seeds)
1 tsp rai (mustard seeds)

METHOD

1 Cut brinjals into half lengthwise then cut each piece diagonally into two pieces. Sprinkle ½ tsp salt. Keep aside for 15 minutes to sweat. Wash well.

2 Heat a kadhai. Reduce heat. Add all collected ingredients together – hing, saunf, kalonji, methi dana and rai. Stir till methi dana turns brown.

3 Add ginger or garlic paste. Stir. Add curry leaves. Stir.

4 Add chopped tomatoes and stir for about 7-8 minutes till dry.

5 Add haldi, red chilli powder, dhania powder, salt and garam masala. Stir.

6 Add baingans. Sprinkle ¼ tsp salt. Cook covered for 15 minutes on slow fire till soft. Serve hot sprinkled with green coriander and garam masala.

Kurkure Bhein

Serves 4

250 gm bhein or kamal kakri (lotus stem)
2 onions - cut into 8 pieces
4 tbsp atta (wheat flour)
some amchoor and garam masala to sprinkle
3 green chillies- keep whole, ½ cup chopped coriander, 1 tbsp lemon juice

OTHER INGREDIENTS
1" piece ginger, 4-5 flakes garlic, 2 green chillies
½ tsp ajwain (carom seeds)
1 tsp lemon juice, 1½ tbsp curd
¾ tsp salt, ½ tsp red chilli powder
½ tsp soya sauce, 1 tbsp tomato ketchup

METHOD

1 Choose thick bhein. Cut bhein diagonally into ½" or ¼" thick, slanting pieces. Wash well. Use a toothpick to clean if it is dirty.

2 Boil in salted water till soft; or pressure cook in 1 cup water to give one whistle. Keep on low flame for 5-7 minutes.

3 Strain the boiled bhein. Dry them well on a kitchen towel.

4 Grind ginger, garlic and green chillies to a paste. Add ajwain, lemon juice, curd, salt and red chilli powder to this paste. Mix well.

5 Apply the paste all over on the bhein. Keep aside for 1 hour.

6 Heat a pan. Reduce flame. Add atta. Cook for ½-1 minute till the atta turns golden brown. Remove from fire. Sprinkle the roasted atta over the marinated bhein to cover completely.

7 Heat a kadhai. Add onions to the kadhai and stir till brown specs appear on them.

8 Add bhein and stir till light brown specs appear on them.

9 Sprinkle ¼ tsp amchoor powder, ¼ tsp garam masala, soya sauce & ketchup. Stir fry for 5-6 minutes till they turn dry and crisp. Add whole green chillies, coriander and lemon juice, mix well.

Note: At the time of buying bhein, see that both the **ends** are **closed.** The closed ends prevent the dirt from going inside. Do not buy very thin bhein.

Spinach Soya Keema

Serves 4

INGREDIENTS

¾ cup soya granules - soak together for 15 minutes
1 cup milk
2 cups spinach (paalak) - shredded
4 mushrooms - grated
3-4 flakes garlic
2-3 sookhi lal mirch (dry red chillies)
1 tsp jeera (cumin seeds)
1 onion - grated
1 tsp ginger - chopped
¼ tsp haldi, 1 tsp dhania powder, 1 tsp salt or to taste, ¼ tsp garam masala
2 tsp lemon juice
seeds of 1 choti illaichi (green cardamom) - powdered

METHOD

1 Shred spinach into thin long pieces. Measure 2 cups of shredded spinach. Wash in several changes of water. Keep aside.

2 Soak soya granules in milk. Keep aside for 15-20 minutes.

3 Crush garlic and dry red chillies together in a small spice grinder.

4 Heat a pan. Add 1 tsp jeera to the pan. Stir for a few seconds till fragrant.

5 Add crushed garlic and red chilli paste. Mix and cook on low heat till garlic turns golden.

6 Add onion, cook till golden brown. Add ginger. Stir.

7 Add grated mushrooms and cook for 2-3 minutes, stirring continuously.

8 Add paalak, haldi, dhania powder, salt & garam masala. Mix well for 2 minutes.

9 Add soaked granules along with the milk. Bhuno for 7-8 minutes till dry.

10 Add lemon juice & powdered chhoti illaichi. Mix well & serve hot.

Tikka Subzi

Serves 6-8

INGREDIENTS

200 gm broccoli (1 small head)
200 gm cauliflower (1 small head) - cut into medium florets
5-6 mushrooms, 50 gm babycorns
2 round slices of pineapple - cut into 1" triangles
1 capsicum green or coloured - cut into fine rings
2 onions - cut into fine rings, 1 tomato - deseeded and cut into triangles
½ tsp ginger paste, few drops lemon juice, ¼ tsp kala namak, ¼ tsp salt

1ST MARINADE
1 tbsp lemon juice, ¾ tsp ajwain (carom seeds), ½ tsp salt

2ND MARINADE
1½ cups thick curd - hang for 15 minutes or more & squeezed to remove all water
1 tbsp cornflour, 1 tbsp ginger-garlic paste
¼ tsp red chilli powder, ½ tsp salt, 1 tsp tandoori masala

METHOD

1 Boil 6 cups of water in a large pan. Add 1 tsp salt , 1 tsp sugar & 1 tsp lemon juice. Add broccoli, cauliflower, mushrooms and babycorns to water. As soon as the boil returns, remove from fire. Drain. Wipe the pieces with a clean kitchen towel or on a paper napkin till well dried.

2 Spread the broccoli, cauliflower, mushrooms & babycorns on a tray & sprinkle the ingredients of the 1st marinade. Marinate the vegetables for 15 minutes.

3 Drain the vegetables of any excess juice.

4 Mix all the ingredients of the 2nd marinade in a large pan/bowl. Add the broccoli, cauliflower, mushrooms and babycorns to it & mix well.

5 Cover the rack with foil. Place the marinated broccoli, cauliflower, mushrooms and babycorns on the foil and bake in preheated oven at 180°C for 15 minutes. Do not over cook as it turns dry. Keep aside

6 Heat a non stick pan. Add chopped pineapple and cook till golden brown. Fry onion and capsicum rings for a few minutes till onions turn transparent.

7 Add ½ tsp ginger paste & a few drops of lemon juice. Add kala namak & salt. Add tomatoes.

8 Add grilled broccoli, cauliflower, mushrooms and babycorns. Toss for a few minutes. Serve hot.

Vegetable Jalfrazie

Serves 4

INGREDIENTS

1 large onion - chopped
3 carrots - cut into 1¼" long, thin fingers
1 capsicum - cut into ½" pieces
1 cup peas (matar) - boiled
3-4 flakes garlic
½" piece ginger - chopped
4 tomatoes - roasted, peeled and chopped
1½ tsp salt, or to taste
1 tbsp readymade tomato puree, 2 tsp vinegar
¾ tsp black pepper powder (kali mirch powder)
1 tsp sugar, 1 tsp oregano
2 tsp cornflour dissolved in ½ cup water

METHOD

1 Pierce a tomato on a fork deeply and hold it over a naked flame for 2-3 minutes to blacken and loosen the skin. Peel and chop the roasted tomatoes.

2 In a kadhai, put the chopped onions, ginger, garlic and carrots. Add ½ cup water and salt.

3 Cook for 7-8 minutes on low heat till the carrots get just done. Do not over cook.

4 Add the chopped tomatoes. Cook for 4-5 minutes.

5 Add tomato puree, vinegar, black pepper powder, oregano and 1 tsp of sugar. Mix well together.

6 Add the boiled peas and capsicum. Mix well.

7 Add cornflour paste and cook till sauce turns thick. Serve hot.

Mili Juli Subzi

Serves 6-8

INGREDIENTS

1 large potato - peeled, scooped to form small balls (about 8 balls)
200 gm (1 packet) baby cabbage or brussel sprouts (15-20 pieces) - trim the stalk end or ½ of a small cabbage - cut into 1" pieces
100 gms baby corns (7-8) - keep whole if small or cut into 2 pieces if big
¼ cup peas (matar), 6-7 French beans - cut into ¼" pieces (½ cup)
1 carrot - cut into ¼" pieces (½ cup)
6-7 baby onions or 1 regular onions - cut into 4 pieces
15 cherry tomatoes or 2 regular small tomatoes - cut into 4, remove pulp
¼ tsp haldi, 1 tsp salt, ½ tsp red chilli powder, ½ tsp garam masala
½ tsp degi mirch

BOILED ONION PASTE
1 onion, 2 laung, seeds of 2 chhoti illaichi (green cardamoms), ½ cup water

TOMATO PASTE (GRIND TOGETHER)
2 tbsp curd, 2 tbsp grated paneer
2 tomatoes - put in boiling hot water for 3-4 minutes and peeled (blanched)

METHOD

1 Make balls of a potato with the help of a melon scooper.

2 Boil potato balls in salted water till just done. Remove from water. Add baby cabbage, baby cors, peas, french beans and carrots. Boil till vegetables are done.

3 For onion paste, boil onions with all the ingredients of onion paste for 3-4 minutes on low heat. Cool and grind to a paste. Keep aside.

4 For masala, heat a kadhai, add onion paste. Stir for a minute on low heat. Add haldi. Mix well.

5 Add tomato paste. Stir for 8-10 minutes till dry.

6 Add salt and red chilli powder. Add ¾ cup water, ½ tsp garam masala and degi mirch. Boil. Cook for ½ a minute.

7 Add boiled vegetables, onions and tomatoes. Mix well for 2-3 minutes. Serve hot garnished with a blanched floret of broccoli.

Chinese and Thai Dishes

Thai Red Curry

A spicy red Thai curry simmered with assorted vegetables. Enjoy it with steamed rice.

Serves 4-6

RED CURRY PASTE
4-5 dry Kashmiri red chillies - soaked in ½ cup warm water for 10 minutes
½ onion - chopped
8-10 flakes garlic - peeled, ½" piece ginger - sliced
1 stalk lemon grass or rind of 1 lemon
1½ tsp coriander seeds (dhania saboot), 1 tsp cumin (jeera) - roasted
6 peppercorns (saboot kali mirch), 1 tsp salt, 1 tbsp lemon juice

VEGETABLES
6-8 baby corns - slit lengthwise
1 long thin brinjal - cut into ½" slices
½ small broccoli - cut into florets, 2-3 mushrooms - sliced
¼ cup chopped bamboo shoots (optional)
3-4 French beans - cut into 2" lengths

OTHER INGREDIENTS
3 cups coconut milk
½ tsp soya sauce, 15 basil leaves - chopped
salt to taste, ½ tsp brown sugar

METHOD

1 Dry roast cumin and coriander on a tawa till fragrant.

2 Grind coriander and cumin with all the other ingredients of the red curry paste along with the water in which the chillies were soaked, to a very smooth paste.

3 Extract 3 cups of coconut milk by soaking grated coconut in 1 cup of warm water. Blend and then strain. Repeat to get 3 cups of milk.

4 Add the red curry paste in a non stick pan & fry for a few seconds on low heat.

5 Add 3-4 tbsp of coconut milk. Add vegetables and cook for 2-3 minutes.

6 Add the rest of the coconut milk, soya sauce and chopped basil leaves.

7 Cover and simmer on low heat for 5-7 minutes till the vegetables are tender.

8 Add salt and sugar to taste. Boil for 1 to 2 minutes. Serve hot with steamed rice or noodles.

Carrot juliennes in Ginger Sauce

Serves 4

INGREDIENTS

3 carrots (gajar)
3 capsicums (simla mirch)
2 tsp ginger paste (fresh)
2 onions - chopped finely
¾ tsp pepper (kali mirch)
1 tsp soya sauce
3 tbsp tomato ketchup
2 tbsp cornflour mixed with ½ cup water
2 vegetable seasoning cubes (maggi, knorr or any other)

METHOD

1 To make stock with cubes, crush 2 vegetable seasoning cubes and mix with 2 cups of water in a saucepan. Give one boil and keep aside.

2 Peel carrots. Wash and cut each into 2 pieces from the center. Cut each piece into thin slices lengthwise. Cut each slice further into very thin fingers to get juliennes or match stick like pieces. Wipe dry on a kitchen towel. Cut capsicum also to get thin fingers.

3 Heat a kadhai. Add onions, cook till golden. Add ginger paste. Stir fry for a few seconds. Add soya sauce, ketchup, carrots and capsicum. Add the prepared stock. Give one boil.

4 Add the cornflour paste. Stir till sauce starts to get thick. Simmer for 1-2 minutes. Serve hot immediately.

Tofu in Hot Garlic Sauce

Serves 2-3

INGREDIENTS

100 gm tofu (paneer can also be used)

GARLIC SAUCE
1½ tbsp garlic - crushed roughly
2 dry, red chillies - deseeded and chopped
¼ onion - chopped (1-2 tbsp)
½ capsicum - cut into tiny cubes (2-3 tbsp)
4½ tbsp tomato ketchup
2 tsp red chilli sauce
2 tsp soya sauce, ½ tsp pepper
1 tsp salt
2 tsp vinegar
¼ tsp ajinomoto (optional)
2 tbsp cornflour mixed with ½ cup water

METHOD

1 To prepare the sauce, peel and grind the garlic to a very rough paste in a small grinder. Keep the mixer on just for 1-2 seconds. Do not make a smooth paste.

2 Heat a pan, remove from fire. Add garlic and red chilli bits. Stir till garlic starts to change its colour.

3 Add onion, cook till soft.

4 Add tomato ketchup, red chilli sauce, soya sauce, pepper and salt. Cook for 1 minute on low heat. Add sugar, vinegar and ajinomoto.

5 Add capsicum.

6 Add 1 cup water, give one boil.

7 Add cornflour paste, stirring all the time. Cook for 2 minutes on low heat. Check salt. Remove from heat. Keep sauce aside.

8 Cut tofu or paneer into 1" cubes or triangles.

9 At serving time, add tofu to sauce and boil for 2 minutes. Serve with rice.

Thai Green Curry

Serves 4

INGREDIENTS

6-8 soya nugget chunks - boiled in 3 cups water for 4-5 minutes or till soft
1 brinjal - cut into slices and sprinkled with salt
50 gm paneer - cut into cubes
½ carrot - diagonally sliced
2½ cups coconut milk, ½ tsp soya sauce, salt, sugar (1 tsp)
10-15 whole basil leaves

GREEN CURRY PASTE

5-6 green chillies - chopped, 1 onion - chopped
stalk of 1 lemon grass or 1 rind of lemon
½ tbsp chopped garlic, ½" piece ginger, ½ tsp salt, ¼ tsp haldi
¼-½ tsp peppercorns (saboot kali mirch)
1 tbsp lemon juice, 1 tbsp coriander seeds (saboot dhania) - roasted
1 tsp cumin seeds (jeera) - roasted, 1 cup basil leaves or coriander leaves and stalks

METHOD

1 For the green curry paste, dry roast coriander and cumin seeds for 2 minutes on a tawa till fragrant but not brown. Put all other ingredients of the curry paste and the roasted seeds in a grinder and grind to a fine paste, using a little water.

2 Add green paste to a pan. Add nuggets and cook for 2-3 minutes on low heat.

3 Wash brinjals and add to the paste. Add carrot also. Stir for 2 minutes.

4 Add salt, sugar and coconut milk. Boil. Add soya sauce. Cover and cook on low heat for a few minutes or till brinjals are well cooked.

5 Add basil, tofu or paneer. Give 2-3 boils. Garnish with sliced red or green chillies (long thin slices), basil leaves. Serve hot with boiled/steamed rice.

Note: You can use vegetables of your choice. Cauliflower, babycorns, french beans, mushrooms can be added at step 3.

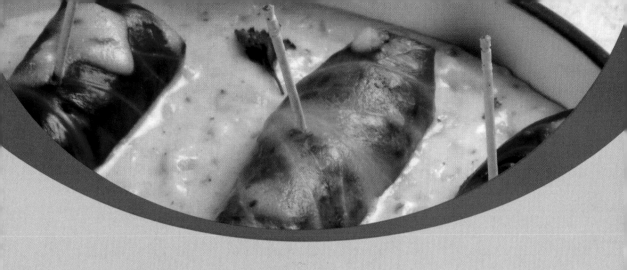

Baked and Continental Dishes

Vegetables in Tomato Basil

Serves 8

INGREDIENTS

150 gm green pumpkin (kadoo) - cut into about 8 thin slices (even less than ¼" thickness)
1 potato - cut into thin round slices, 100 gm paneer - cut into triangles
½ cup milk
4 bread slices - ground to get fresh bread crumbs
1 tsp oregano, ¼ tsp salt, ¼ tsp pepper

TOMATO SAUCE

1 kg tomatoes – blanch and chop 250 gm and puree the other 750 gm
1 onion - chopped finely, 3-4 flakes garlic - crushed (½ tsp)
1 tbsp maida mixed with ½ cup water to a paste
10-12 whole basil leaves or 2-3 tbsp of finely chopped coriander leaves
1 tsp dried oregano, ½ tsp pepper, ½ tsp red chilli flakes or ¼ tsp chilli powder
½ tsp honey, ¾ tsp salt or to taste

TOPPING & FILLING

1 tbsp corn kernels, ½ capsicum - cut into tiny cubes, 1 tsp paneer - grated

METHOD

1 Boil 5-6 cups water with 1 tsp salt and 2 tbsp lemon juice. Add pumpkin and potato slices to the boiling water and boil for 3-4 minutes or till soft.

2 Mix bread crumbs with 1 tsp oregano, ¼ tsp salt & pepper. Spread on a plate.

3 Dip the pumpkin, potato and paneer slices in milk and then press on bread crumbs scattered on a plate. Turn side to coat both sides. Brown on a greased non stick pan, turning sides, to make them light brown on both sides. Remove from pan. Keep aside.

4 For the tomato sauce, blanch the tomatoes by putting them in hot water for 4-5 minutes. Remove from water and peel. Chop 250 gm & puree the remaining.

5 In a kadhai, put the onions with ½ tsp salt and saute for 2-3 minutes on low flame till slightly soft. Add garlic. Stir. Add the chopped and pureed tomatoes, oregano, pepper, chilli flakes and honey. Cook for 4-5 minutes. Add maida paste and stir for 1-2 minutes. Boil. Simmer for 2 minutes. Add basil. Cook for a minute. Remove from fire.

6 Spread some prepared tomato sauce in a large flat dish or platter which is heat proof. Place pumpkin, potato and paneer slices on it in separate rows.

7 Spread some prepared tomato sauce over the slices. Top with some corn, capsicum and finely grated paneer.

8 To serve, bake just for 10 minutes at 200°C/400°F till hot enough to serve.

Veggies Baked in Green Sauce

Serves 5-6

INGREDIENTS

4-6 baby corns - sliced into 2 lengthways
1 carrot - peeled and cut into diagonal slices and then cut into thin strips ¼" broad
1½ cups of small florets of cauliflower, ¼ cup peas, frozen or boiled
75 gm mushrooms - cut the stem into round slices & the top into 2 pieces horizontally
½ cup whole wheat pasta, optional
1 tomato - cut into 4 pieces, deseeded and cut into thin long pieces
1- 2 slices of fresh pineapple

GREEN PASTE

1 onion - chopped finely, 2 tbsp milk, 1 tsp garlic paste
1½ cups chopped spinach, ½ tsp each - salt, pepper and oregano

OTHER INGREDIENTS FOR SAUCE

3 tbsp whole wheat flour (atta), 2 cups milk

TOPPING

2" piece paneer- grated (1-2 tbsp)

METHOD

1. Boil 3-4 cups water with 1 tsp salt, 1 tsp sugar and 1 tsp lemon juice. Add vegetables and boil for 1 minute. Remove from water with a strainer.

2. Add salt to the water again. Add pasta. Boil for 12-15 minutes, or till soft. Strain and keep aside.

3. Heat a nonstick pan. Put pineapple slices. Brown both sides lightly. Cut into pieces. Add the blanched veggies to the pan. Saute for 1-2 minutes till crisp tender. Remove from pan and keep aside.

4. To prepare sauce, put 2 tbsp milk add the garlic and onion in a pan. Stir on low flame. Saute for a minute and add spinach. Saute for 5 minutes. Add salt, pepper and oregano. Remove from fire and let it cool. Blend to a green puree with a little water. Keep aside.

5. Add whole wheat flour in a kadhai and cook on low flame for 1-2 minutes. Add spinach puree and stir for 2 minutes. Remove from fire.

6. Gradually add milk, stirring continuously.

7. Return to fire. Boil, stirring. Reduce heat and check salt, pepper. Mix well for a minute or till it starts to coat the back of a spoon.

8. Add veggies and pasta. Bring to a boil. Add tomato slices & pineapple pieces. Mix. Remove from fire.

9. Take an oven proof dish. Transfer the veggies in it. Sprinkle grated paneer over the veggies. Bake at 180°C for 20 minutes.

Vegetable Au Gratin

Serves 4

INGREDIENTS

½ cup shelled peas
1 cup tiny florets (½-¼" pieces) of cauliflower
or
1 small potato - cut into ¼" squares
6-7 french beans - finely chopped (1/3 cup)
2 carrots - cut into ¼" squares (1 cup)

SAUCE
2½ tbsp cornflour, 2½ cups milk
2 tbsp chopped coriander
½ onion - very finely chopped
¾ tsp salt, ¾ tsp tomato ketchup

CRUSH TOGETHER
1 green chilli - deseeded and finely chopped, 2 flakes garlic
½ tsp saboot kali mirch (peppercorns)

METHOD

1 Thread beans. Peel carrots & potatoes. Cut all vegetables into small pieces.

2 Cut cauliflower into small florets without stem.

3 Wash all vegetables together.

4 Remove from water & put in a pressure cooker. Add ¼ cup water & ½ tsp salt. Mix well.

5 Pressure cook to give 1 whistle. Remove from fire. Immediately put the cooker in the sink and put under water to release steam. This prevents the vegetables from being overcooked. Keep cooker aside.

6 Crush together green chillies, garlic and peppercorns to a rough paste.

7 Mix cornflour with ½ cup milk to a smooth paste.

8 Mix the rest of the milk with all ingredients of the sauce together in a heavy bottomed pan. Add the crushed paste and the cornflour paste to it. Keep on fire. Boil. Cook stirring continuously till it boils and starts to coat the spoon.

9 Add the vegetables along with the water if any. Cook for 4-5 minutes on high flame, stirring continuously till the sauce gets thick again. Remove from fire. Add more salt if required.

10 Transfer to a greased oven proof dish and bake in a hot oven at 200°C for about 15-20 minutes or till light brown.

Cabbage Rolls In White Sauce

Serves 12

INGREDIENTS

5 cabbage leaves - outer leaves
1 cup sprouts (preferably moth dal), 4 tbsp worcestershire sauce
a small boiled & grated potato, 6-8 jalapeno slices - finely chopped
1 tsp ginger - chopped, ½ tsp salt, white pepper, to taste

WHITE SAUCE
½ onion - finely chopped, ¼ tsp garlic paste
2 tbsp atta (whole wheat flour), 1 tsp chopped coriander, ½ tsp salt
½ tsp red chilli flakes, ½ tsp white pepper, 1½ cups milk, 1 tsp tomato ketchup

METHOD

1 Cut the lower center portion of the cabbage leaf which is hard in an (^) inverted "V" manner. Now it becomes easier to roll the leaf.

2 Boil 4-5 cups some water and 1 tsp each of salt, sugar and lemon juice to it. Bring to boil and add cabbage leaves to it.

3 Blanch the cabbage leaves for 4-5 minutes till soft. Remove from water and keep aside.

4 Heat a pan. Add chopped ginger to it. Stir for a few seconds.

5 Add sprouts and worcestershire sauce. Cook covered till sprouts turn tender. Add grated potato & jalapenos to it. Mix well.

6 Season the mixture with white pepper and salt.

7 Now take a cabbage leaf, put a spoon full of mix at the edge, leaving 1" and roll it nicely till the end. Secure with a tooth pick

8 Pan fry the rolls on greased pan on very low heat till light brown patches appear.

9 Mix all the above ingredients of white sauce together with whisk to get a smooth mixture.

10 Cook it on medium flame, stirring continuously to get a saucy consistency.

11 Spread most of the white sauce in an oven proof dish and place the cabbage rolls on it.

12 Pour the remaining sauce on top and grate some paneer on it. Grill for 5-7 minutes. Serve hot.

Cream Free Desserts
&
Drinks

Fruit Magic

Can be served as a dessert or a filler when you are hungry.

Makes 2

INGREDIENTS

1 kiwi - chopped and blended with lots of ice cubes and artificial sweetener if needed
½ cup chopped pineapple - blended with lots of ice cubes and artificial sweetener if needed
½ cup chopped strawberries or watermelon - blended with a few ice cubes, a pinch of salt (optional) and artificial sweetener if needed

METHOD

1 Keep kiwi puree, pineapple puree and strawberry or watermelon puree separately in a bowl.

2 Using a spoon, gently put the heaviest (kiwi) fruit puree first. Then add the pineapple one and lastly put the lightest one.

Lite Cafe Shake

Makes 2 Glasses

INGREDIENTS

1 cup cold lite (toned) milk
3 tsp coffee, 1 cup diet coke
lots of ice, some cocoa to sprinkle

METHOD

1 Blend milk, ice and coffee till frothy. Add 1 cup coke and blend again. Pour in a glass. Sprinkle a pinch of cocoa on it. Serve as an evening or breakfast shake.

Seb (Apple) Ka Meetha

Serves 8

INGREDIENTS

2 apples - grated with the peel

SUGAR SYRUP
¼ cup sugar, ¼ cup water
seeds of 4-5 chhoti ilaichi - crushed
2 drops kewra essence

KESARI MILK
3 cups milk
¼ tsp saffron (kesar)
3 tbsp sugar
1 cup milk mixed with 2 tbsp cornflour

OTHER INGREDIENTS
1 apple - grated with the peel
2-3 almonds and 2-3 kishmish - chopped
seeds of 2-3 chhoti illaichi - crushed

METHOD

1 For the sugar syrup, put sugar, water and illaichi in a kadhai. Bring to a boil. Simmer on low heat for 2-3 minutes.

2 To the syrup, add 2 grated apples. Cook for 3-4 minutes till dry. Add kewra essence and mix well.

3 For the kesari milk, boil milk with kesar in a clean kadhai.

4 Add sugar and reduce heat. Simmer for 15 minutes till it is reduced to about ½ the quantity. Do not let it get thick.

5 Add cornflour dissolved in milk. Bring to a boil, stirring constantly. Cook for 2-3 minutes on low heat till thick.

6 Add the sweetened apples. Cook till quite thick. Remove from fire.

7 Grate 1 apple and spread a layer of grated apple at the base of a medium size serving dish.

8 Pour the apples in milk over it & spread. Sprinkle some illaichi powder & chopped nuts. Keep in the fridge for 2-3 hours to set. Serve cold garnished with rose petals.

Fruit Parfait

Serves 6

INGREDIENTS

1 cup yogurt - hang for 30 minutes in a muslin cloth
2 cups chopped papaya
¼ cup milk
¼ tsp vanilla essence
3 tbsp powdered sugar or 3 tablets artificial sweetener
¼ cup anar ke dane
1-2 slices of fresh ripe pineapple
2 kiwi fruit - peeled and chopped
½ cup sliced strawberries
2 tbsp strawberry crush or syrup - to coat the glasses
a big apple - for decoration

METHOD

1 Put papaya in a mixer. Blend till smooth. Cook this papaya puree for 3-4 minutes on medium flame. Keep aside to cool.

2 Put hung yogurt, cooked papaya puree, milk and vanilla essence in the blender and blend again. Check and add sugar or artificial sweetener to taste. Keep papaya whip aside.

3 Coat a narrow glass with ½ tsp of strawberry syrup or crush. Put 1 tbsp anar ke dane.

4 Arrange a layer of chopped pineapple pieces.

5 Put 1" layer of papaya whip.

6 Arrange some kiwi and strawberries along the sides of the wall.

7 Put a layer of whip again. Keep in the fridge.

8 At serving time, top with 3-4 thin, tall pieces of apple slices with the peel. Drizzle some crush on them. Serve.

Orange Rabri

Bread is used to thicken milk. Orange rind makes a great combination.
Serves 4

INGREDIENTS

1 kg toned milk
seeds of 2-3 chhoti illaichi (green cardamom) - crushed
1 slice bread - sides removed & ground to crumbs in a mixer
2-3 tbsp sugar
1" fresh orange peel, scrape white pith - cut into thread fine strips and chop

ORANGE TOPPING
5 gm (½ packet) agar agar (china grass) - soaked in 1 cup ready made orange juice for 15 minutes
1 tbsp sugar
1 large orange - peeled & skin removed

METHOD

1 Place milk and illaichi in a kadhai. Boil. Simmer for 30 minutes on low heat.

2 Add fresh bread crumbs. Cook for about 10 minutes till slightly thick like rabri. Add sugar to taste. Mix and remove from heat. Add orange peel.

3 Heat soaked agar agar on low heat, for 4-5 minutes (do not boil), till it melts completely. Remove from fire and wait for 1 minute.

4 Put half of the rabri into a shallow serving dish.

5 Pour half of the orange topping over it. Keep in the freezer for 5 minutes or till it sets slightly.

6 Spread the remaining rabri on the topping.

7 Top rabri with the left over orange topping. Garnish with peeled orange segments or rind.

Note: The orange topping has china grass which sets at room temperature. So if the 2nd batch of topping starts to set before it is poured, you can reheat it slightly.

Cafe Coke magic

Serves 6-8

INGREDIENTS

½ tin milkmaid, 4 tsp gelatine
2 cups sweet, fresh curd - hang for 30 minutes, ½ tsp vanilla essence, ½ cup diet coke

COFFEE SAUCE
1 cup water, 4 tsp cocoa, 4 tsp coffee, 6 tsp cornflour
¼ cup sugar or 7 tablets or 5 sachets of artificial sweetener

CHOCOLATE SAUCE
¼ cup water, 1 tsp cornflour, 1 tsp coffee, 2 tablets or sugar to taste

OTHER INGREDIENTS
2-3 kiwis - cut into half slices, few orange segments, 1-2 strawberries - sliced

METHOD

1 Sprinkle gelatine on ¼ cup water kept in a small heavy bottomed pan. Let it stand for a minute. Heat on very low flame till completely dissolved. Do not boil.

2 Mix all ingredients of the coffee sauce, except sweetener, with a whisk. Keep stirring continuously on medium heat till it attains a coating consistency. Remove from fire. Add sugar.

3 Add the gelatine solution to the coffee sauce, stirring continuously. Add essence. Let it cool down. In summers put it in the fridge.

4 Beat dahi till very smooth in a blender. Add condensed milk to curd and beat some more.

5 Add the cooled coffee sauce to the condensed milk mixture.

6 Add coke. Mix well and check for sweetness. Add more if needed. (it depends on the dahi that you use)

7 Mix all ingredients except artificial sweetner of the chocolate sauce in a small heavy bottom pan till smooth. Keep on low heat till it coats the spoon. Remove from fire and let it cool to room temperature.

8 Coat a bowl with a few lines of chocolate sauce lines.

9 Pour half of the dessert in the bowl and keep in the freezer to set. Keep the remaining dessert aside in the fridge.

10 Arrange sliced kiwis along the sides of the bowl on the set dessert. Put more fruits on the dessert.

11 Pour the remaining mixture over the fruits & keep in the freezer to set.

12 Sprinkle cocoa powder on the set dessert. Pour the sauce in circles and top with a strawberry.

13 Just 15 minutes before serving, put it in the freezer so that it is properly chilled when served.

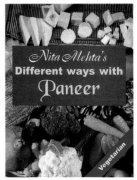

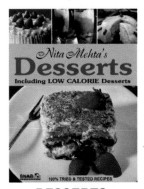

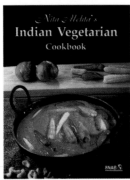

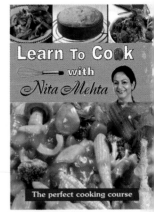